POEMS FROM THE
POLKA-DOT APOCALYPSE

J. Martin Strangeweather

All rights reserved. No part of this book may be reproduced or transmitted in any form or by any means, electronic or mechanical, without written permission from the author. All requests should be sent to: jmartinstrangeweather@gmail.com

Cover artwork by J. Martin Strangeweather
Published by Four Feathers Press
Printed in the United States of America
© 2021 by J. Martin Strangeweather

for all the ghosts who still hunger

Tears of Osiris: A Recipe for Disaster

Take one fundamental thread of Creation and stretch it across eternity, laying out the tripwire. Then wait patiently. It might take an infinity or two, but something will eventually come along and spring the mechanism, triggering the formation of a universe. Wondering who or what trips the wire is a fool's game. In some form or another, the answer always ends up being you. You're the one who's to blame for this mess, and forgetfulness is no excuse for leniency. Allow the newly formed universe a fraction of a second to cool, then strain the leftover matter from the antimatter, regulating gravity. Adjust the frequency setting until you find a stable quantum of electromagnetic action. Settings may vary from universe to universe. After stabilizing the cosmological substratum, calibrate the energy distribution matrix to $E = mc^2$ and set the subatomic particles aside for approximately five hundred million years, allowing the mixture enough time to congeal into stars and galaxies. Once the first batch of stars begins to go supernova, stir in the remaining elements and let the universe simmer for an additional ten billion years, occasionally checking for signs of life. Remember, in order to destroy your enemies, you must first create them. When programming rudimentary biological algorithms, it's important not to confuse DNA codes with RNA codes. Also, during the early phase of biospheric construction, be sure not to mistake the greenish blue algae button for the bluish green mold button, or the violet wire for the ultraviolet wire. Try not to get your wires crossed in general. The initial development of life requires infernal conditions. You were born from seas of magma and rivers of hellfire, cataclysmic earthquakes, poisonous sulfuric clouds. Once the earliest multicellular lifeforms take shape, soak the biosphere in primal fear for two to three billion years. Evolution may vary from biosphere to biosphere. At the first sign of civilization, pour in a liberal dose of greed and sprinkle with shame. Wait approximately ten thousand years for modernity to occur, then massacre eleven million Native American Indians, exterminate six million Jews, execute two million Cambodians, butcher one million Armenians, slaughter eight hundred thousand Rwandans, eradicate seven hundred thousand Australian aborigines, and drop two atomic bombs that wipe out two hundred thousand Japanese civilians. Intentionally starve fifteen million Hindus, three million North Koreans, and one million Tibetans. Enslave three million Africans in the name of *life, liberty, and the pursuit of happiness* knowing full well that *all men are created equal*. Collect the blood and tears resulting from these atrocities and use the accursed liquid to marinate humanity's collective unconscious for seven to ten generations, until irreparable psychogenetic damage occurs, transforming every thought, every utterance, and every perception into something monstrous, manufacturing a zombified world of radioactive oceans under X-ray skies, everything you touch… contaminated… with tiny invisible monsters. Increase the level of dishonesty to a billion lies per second and check frequently for mass extinction while chanting, "The fragrant lotus only grows from the muck of the swamp," and praying for all the sour grapes to rot into heady wine.

Commencement Speech

Maybe we should strive to be average.

No pressure to excel or shine brighter than
your neighbors, coworkers, and competitors.

No pressure to be faster, more efficient.

No desperation to be wealthy, wealthier, wealthie$$$t.

To be okay with yourself and where you are
instead of always feeling like you're behind.

To clock out at five and spend the rest of the day
not caring.

To abide rather than win.

legacy

the interviewer asked
what do you want your legacy to be

i came from language
and to language
i shall return

what more
could i
should i
possibly expect

what legacy have i inherited from my ancestors
from *homo erectus*
i inherited the ability to walk upright
from *homo ergaster*
i inherited the knowledge of taming fire

what sort of collective legacy will our current incarnation
hand down to future generations
a million years from now
a mere ten thousand
many can't even imagine
how the human race is going to survive
the next one hundred

put simply
i hope to give back more than i have taken
but i'm worried this is impossible
without a radical shift
in my consumer behavior

(On a less altruistic note, I would like to be remembered as the Poet Laureate of the Surreal, the Bizarre. The Poet Laureate of Forgotten Deities and Secret Passageways. Or how about the Poet Laureate of Failure? That's more honest. The Poet Laureate of Loneliness. Maybe the Poet Laureate of Worming Paranoia—of Madness Used as a Tool! The Poet Laureate of Delusion, Hypocrisy, and the Seven Deadly Sins!)

wouldn't it be nice

if

after my eventual assassination

someone erected a statue in my honor

not too tall

ten feet would suffice

but the statue should be a robot

or golem of some sort

the automaton would lumber around the city

fixing potholes and rescuing cats stuck in trees

perhaps the automaton would start a book club

or

maybe the mayor could erect a hundred-foot-tall statue

of me

carved entirely out of soap

my legacy would melt at the first real downpour

cleansing the streets

delicate bubbles rising to the heavens

for a passing child's delight

in the untamable

unnamable

future

i merely wish

as most folks do

for history's severe lens

to cast me in a brighter light

than the shadows with which i associate myself

Everyman the Liar

Evil has the power
To do
What others will not.
Goodness seeks safety
In transparent numbers.

Peaceful protests
And armchair activism
Have no effect
On those without conscience.

Do you want to fix the problem
Or punish the wrongdoers?
Rarely are the two synonymous.

Do you stalk
Everyone you meet
Online?

If you want to make the world a better place,
Remember to start with yourself.
I think Gandhi said that,
Or maybe it was Michael Jackson.

Behind every innovative genius who died penniless
Is a shortsighted gatekeeper who didn't understand,
Wouldn't get past their own pettiness,
Couldn't see beyond their own vanity.

Everyone knows the difference between right and wrong
Until their job or reputation is at risk.
All of our evils boil down to pride and greed.

Which is more important—
Justice, or keeping the peace?
Rarely are the two synonymous.

The human race will eventually become extinct
Because some of us never learned
To play nice.

Hamster Wheel

All the movies have already been watched.
All the amusement park rides have already been ridden.

The races have all been run.
The products have all been bought
And sold.

All the backs have been stabbed.
All the books have been written.
All the words . . . spoken.
All the thoughts . . . thought.

Hamster wheel,
Hamster wheel,
Remember a time before stars.
You are not these things.
You are nothing more than these things.
But what could this mean?

Your chair is made of eggshells,
Your bed is made of salted wounds,
Dresser full of Freudian slips and secondhand dreams,
Uniforms fashioned from broken mirrors,
None of which reflect you,
While the clock whispers lies.

All the lives have already been lived.
All the gods have already been invented.

Hamster wheel galaxy
In the fractal lingua-verse,
Spin me a web
To call home.

Typical Day 2020

Wear a facemask.
Wash your hands.
Do not touch anything.
Do not touch anyone.
Do not leave your house.
Do not trust the news.
Do not trust the police.
Do not trust the government.

Our neighbors are mirrors
Through which we catch distrustful glimpses
Of ourselves.

Stock up on toilet paper.
Wash your hands again, just to be safe.
Fill the bathtub with antibacterial gel.
Do not trust your own eyes and ears.
Seriously consider buying a firearm.

Too Much Butter, Not Enough Bread

I lived in a cave during the winter of 2019
Never once wandering into the daylight
Took a vow of silence that year
Memorized 10,000 Buddhist sutras
Quit eating carbohydrates
Swore off meat and dairy
Fasted for six months
Surviving on ten sunflower seeds
And a cupped handful of water per day
Until I almost died

For all the good it did
I should have volunteered to work
At the local soup kitchen

Twelve-Step Program

January: I'm starting to question the motives of my toothpaste. I wonder if it really has my best interest in mind.

February: I'm starting to question the motives of the FDA. I wonder if they really have my best interest in mind.

March: I'm starting to question the motives of my smartphone. I wonder if it really has my best interest in mind.

April: I'm starting to question the motives of my newsfeed. I wonder if it really has my best interest in mind.

May: I'm starting to question the motives of my neighbors. I wonder if they really have my best interest in mind.

June: I'm starting to question the motives of my friends and family. I wonder if they really have my best interest in mind.

July: I'm starting to question the motives of teachers, doctors, repairmen, and businesspeople in general. I wonder if they really have my best interest in mind.

August: I'm starting to question the motives of my supervisor. I wonder if he really has my best interest in mind.

September: I'm starting to question the motives of my religion. I wonder if it really has my best interest in mind.

October: I'm starting to question the motives of my president. I wonder if he really has my best interest in mind.

November: I'm starting to question the motives of my spouse. I wonder if they really have my best interest in mind.

December: I'm starting to question my own motives. I wonder if I really have my best interest in mind.

Everything We Know About Ducks Thus Far

1. If it looks like a duck and acts like a duck, it's a duck.

2. If we believe it looks like a duck and we believe it acts like a duck, let's treat it as a duck, for now.

3. A duck is a bird is a drake is a mallard is a member of the species *Anas platyrhynchos* is an image in a wildlife magazine is a rubber toy in a bathtub is a pet named Bill is dinner is dung.

4. A duck could in fact be an eagle, in which case eagles would be referred to as ducks.

5. A duck is the experience of duckness, as defined by one's culture.

6. A duck is the sum of its functions, which are too innumerable to list.

7. A duck is anything that remains after every instance of non-duck has been eliminated from consideration.

8. The mallard you are experiencing (via semantic, representational, and psychological software, which combined transmit an estimated 11,000,000 bits of data per second into your cerebral hardware, though only 60 bits per second become processed into conscious awareness) resulted from your initial observation of the aforementioned duck, which collapsed the multiversal wave function (i.e., the hyperspatially entangled quantum superposition of identical yet probabilistically differentiated versions of the mallard in numerous alternate worlds occupying numerous alternate universes, doing every possible thing a mallard can do, being in every possible state a mallard can undergo), tuning one of numerous mallard scenarios into your particular wavelength of the multiverse—your specific experience of reality.

9. Sometimes explaining a duck is like chasing a wild goose.

10. *Quack!*

Lessons Learned

Socrates taught me that everything is false.
Buddha taught me that everyone is sick.
Confucius taught me that everyone has forgotten
Their role.
Moses taught me that everyone is lost
And searching for a home.
Jesus taught me that everyone will fail.
Muhammad taught me that everyone needs
To humble themselves.
Einstein taught me that everything is relative.

Birth taught me how to cry.
Language taught me how to lie.
School taught me how to rebel.
Work taught me how to cooperate.
Pain taught me how to love.
Defeat taught me how to learn.
Death taught me how to live.

Today's History Lesson:

The limit of my mind is the limit of my body.
The limit of my body is the limit of my universe.
The limit of my universe is the limit of my language.
The limit of my language is the limit of my mind.

I am a perceptual field given expression
Through the context of a body.

Pharaoh Ramesses the Third was betrayed by his concubines, who reputedly slit his throat. Julius Caesar was stabbed twenty-three times by the senators of Rome. Caligula was stabbed thirty times to end his bloody reign. Pretty much every Roman emperor met their end by assassination. Makes you wonder what the appeal of so much power was.

The world speaks through hearts.
Hearts speak through dreams.
Dreams speak through prophets.
Prophets speak through poems.

The dream of the world
Is spoken through the poem
In the heart of the prophet.

Emperor Fu Sheng was tied to the end of a horse and dragged through the streets. Vlad the Impaler was cut to pieces and his head was given to his enemy as a gift. King Henry the Third of France was gutted like a fish by a messenger. King Charles the First of England had his head lopped off with an axe for treason. Tsar Nicholas the Second was shot, ran through with bayonets, and burned, along with his family. King Louis the Sixteenth and Marie Antoinette were beheaded by guillotine. Benito Mussolini was shot to death by a firing squad and then hung on a meat hook in the town square for everyone to spit upon. Hitler blew his brains out in a bunker before anyone else could get to him.

Our history lessons are written in blood
On parchments of human flesh,
And every century teaches the same despairing lesson:
If you spill enough innocent blood
Into the scales of justice,
It will eventually tip against the favor of gold,
But only for a short while.

Igneous Prophet

Today I met a man who only spoke in stones.

Pebbles dribbled from his craggy lips
With promises of boulders.

Despite my disbelief,
I will soon be crushed
Beneath his mountain of rubble.

Strange Weather

Stranger things than true love have happened in the USA. Flightless animals have rained from the sky, usually amphibians. Frogs bombarded Kansas City in 1873 and Dubuque in 1882. A deluge of toads blanketed Minneapolis in 1901. Sacramento experienced a downpour of salamanders in 1870. Memphis witnessed a rainfall of black snakes in 1877. Tangles of worms drizzled over Jennings in 2007. Various types of fish showered Cambridge in 1828, Kershaw County in 1901, Marksville in 1947, and Norfolk in the year 2000. Certain fruits have also fallen from the heavens. Unripe peaches plummeted from branchless heights onto Shreveport in 1961, and a hailstorm of green apples pelted Coventry in 2011. Stranger still, cotton candy clouds sprinkled Lake County with sugar crystals twice in 1857.

Strangeweather

The cityscape is a hodgepodge of skyscrapers designed to look like wine bottles and martini glasses and nosebleed stiletto-heel shoes, all constructed from the recycled dreams of dead rock stars. Banana airplanes glide through the sky on glittery feathered wings, and every Christmas Eve the pink cotton candy clouds rain psychedelic gumdrops.

Freshly gutted pigs, sheep, and sasquatches are displayed on meat hooks along the alleyway leading to my high-rise coffin. I reside in a replica of the Statue of Liberty, way up at the top, in the torch. The building's doorman is a life-size bronze statue of the prior doorman, who worked here for fifty years before he was killed in a doorman-related incident.

The penthouse suite (where I kick up my feet) is ultra-intrauterine, with sky blue carpeting and fluffy white pillow-clouds shaped like couches and recliners, wallpapered in silver-lined dove wings. Two wide-eyed windows afford a panoramic view of gargantuan maggots burrowing through cerebral convolutions of bruise-colored firmament.

My refrigerator is stuffed with roadkill marinated in Dom Pérignon. My toilet is made of cholla cactus…
my bathroom mirror is made of yellow misaligned teeth… closetful of fizzled neon Narnia. If you lift up the carpet in the left corner of my bedroom, there's a knothole in the fleshwood floorboard where you can peek at the kaleidoscopic clockwork of the universe within me.

J. Martin Strangeweather is a poet, a painter, a teller of tall tales, and the Chief Executive Prognosticator & Oneiric Director of Thaumaturgic Research for the Santa Ana Literary Association. He graduated from UC Irvine's MFA program in English and Fiction, also earning degrees in Philosophy and Art History. Magister Strangeweather resides in a secret little art colony somewhere in Southern California, where he teaches ornithologists how to sing the language of the birds.

www.ingramcontent.com/pod-product-compliance
Lightning Source LLC
Chambersburg PA
CBHW032019290426
44109CB00013B/720